MW01138664

HENRY WINKLER

The Biography

University Press

Copyright © 2023 University Press

All Rights Reserved

CONTENTS

INTRODUCTION

With everyone dressed up in their evening best, the two comedians Michael Che and Colin Jost spoke loudly from the stage to the crowd attending the 2018 Emmys. After announcing the category and starting the short introductions of the nominees for the award, a speaker came on and announced the two presenters, Claire Foy and Matt Smith. Upon reaching the mic, they expressed how thrilled they were to be presenting the award. Tongue in cheek, Foy said, "If we don't sound thrilled, that's just because we're very, very British." Smith leans forward and says, "Very true. And the Emmy goes to..." They both look down at the card, reading who the winner was, with looks of delight on their faces. Foy then looks up and says, as if it should be obvious, "Henry Winkler."

The camera moves over to the actor who has been a part of daytime TV since the 1970s. The first thing he did was to lean over and kiss his wife. Then he stood and hugged Bill Hader, who hired him for the role that won him the award. Upon reaching the stage, he warmly greeted the announcers. Finally turning to the mic, he gave a comedic, yet hilarious speech.

"Ok. I only have 37 seconds. I wrote this 43 years ago. Can I just say Skip Brittenham said to me a long time ago, if you stay at the table long enough, the chips come to you. And tonight, I got to clear the table. If you get a chance to work with Bill Hader or Alec Berg, run, don't walk. Thank you for producing us, for creating us, for directing us. And Bill for acting with us. And all of our wonderful writers. Sherry Thompson and wonderful Sharon. Sheri Goldberg, an extraordinary publicist. Cliff Aaron, and Chris, who represent me, almost for the first time, I feel represented. I can't stop yet. My wife Stacy. Oh my God, my cast and crew. And the kids – kids – Jed, Zoe, and Max, you can go to bed now. Daddy won!"

The last part of the speech wrapped back around to his having written the speech years ago because by 2018, all of his children were grown up, not young kids who had stayed up with a babysitter, the way the speech made it sound. The people in the crowd all looked incredibly pleased as well, even those who were nominated in the same category. Even though he was up against people like Alec Baldwin and Keenan Thompson, two people who are more familiar to younger generations today, they seemed pleased to see Winkler walk away with the award.

After more than two decades in TV, it was the first time that he had actually won the prestigious award. The joy and happiness on his face as he stood in front of the crowd was very much aligned with his most iconic role – The Fonz. Finally, someone who had helped to influence audiences around the world for decades was gaining some of the recognition he had earned a long time ago.

CHAPTER 1

A lot of the early influence on Winkler's life began in 1930s Germany. His parents, Ilse Anna Marie and Harry Irving Winkler, were Jewish Germans who lived in Berlin at a time when Jews were getting increasingly blamed for all of the problems in the country. As the Nazis gained in popularity, they started to force anyone with Jewish ancestry into increasingly smaller areas, which today are called slums. Toward the end of the 1930s, all Jewish people were moved from the slums into concentration camps. With the oppression going from cohesive control to being outright violent, the Winklers realized that they needed to leave the country. Since it was becoming increasingly more difficult for Jewish people to leave the country easily, Winkler made it seem that he and his wife were traveling abroad for business. It was supposed to be a six-week trip, and one of their brothers, Helmut, was initially supposed to go with him. Unfortunately, Helmut's decision to stay resulted in him being one of the millions of people murdered during the Holocaust.

When discussing it decades later, Henry talked about how his parents were able to leave, "At the time, my father, Harry, told my mother, Ilse, that they were traveling to the US on a brief business trip. He knew they were never going back. Had he told my mother that they were leaving Germany for good, she might have insisted on remaining behind with her family. Many in their families who stayed perished during the Holocaust." The reason their escape was even possible was because he owned a business, and that gave him a valid reason to leave without seeming suspicious to the German authorities. The fact that they had so many family members who remained behind may have also made it feel like the small nuclear family would return to Germany. A large percentage of Jewish Germans who fled took as many family members as possible, so the business trip likely looked legitimate to the people watching his family closely. It doesn't seem that it took long after leaving Germany for his father to tell his mother that they were not going to return to the country.

Figuring he would be able to re-establish himself in the US, Henry Winker's father made sure to collect everything prior to leaving. Since he was the only one who knew that they were leaving permanently, Mr. Winkler took all of his wife's jewelry and hid it so that no one would realize that they were traveling with a lot of money. Since hiding jewelry wasn't exactly easy, he thought of a unique way of making sure no one would suspect anything. Purchasing a box of different chocolates, the older Winkler removed the chocolate from the box and started melting it. While the box was empty, he placed the jewelry in it, then he poured the melted chocolate over it. As they passed through the patrols on the way out of the country, Mr. Winkler made sure to carry the box under his arm. When the Nazis asked if they were leaving the country with anything of significant value, Mr. Winkler said that they could check his bags and see that they have nothing with them.

Upon their arrival in New York City, the clever man sold the jewelry that he had brought with him, giving him ample funds to start a new life with his wife. They weren't nearly so well off as they had been in Germany, but they weren't entirely without money like so many of those who fled Europe were. He had to periodically request that his visa get extended, and the US always approved their request. Whether this was because they knew that the couple was likely to be killed or not is uncertain – the officials did not explain their reasons. However, Harry Winkler was a successful businessman in Germany, which likely made it easier to approve his stay as he was seen as being potentially more valuable with his business acumen.

Just a few years later, they had established

themselves within the US and started to grow their family. Their eldest child was Beatrice Winkler. In 1945, they had their second child, whom they named Henry. It seemed that the children often heard about the events that led to their birth in the country at a time of turmoil in Europe, and it is a story that he has told many times over the years during many interviews. Yet, he still remains aware of how fortunate they were, during an interview with Terry Gross in April 2019, he said at the end of the story, "And I was born, and thank God, 'cause I love our country." Since he was born in the US, that meant Winkler was a natural US citizen, and he would go on to play one of the most iconic American characters in television history.

CHAPTER 2

S ettled into a part of Manhattan, the Winklers had their son on October 30, 1945, only a few months after the defeat of the Germans in Europe and roughly a month after Japan's defeat in Asia. They named him Henry Franklin Winkler and have said that the H in his name is in honor of his Uncle Helmut, who died in the Holocaust. His middle name was to honor Franklin Delano Roosevelt, who was one of the major reasons that Germany was defeated. Uncle Helmut had stayed behind in Germany, hoping to get a dinner jacket from a tailor, and he was going to follow them the next day. Instead, the Nazis took him and moved him into a concentration camp. His family later learned that he ended up in Auschwitz, where he did not survive. Perhaps because the name Helmut was too German, which would have caused problems at a time when there was significant anti-German sentiment, they opted for the name Henry for their son. It's possible that this influenced their expectations of him, wanting their son to be as capable as his other relatives, or as inspirational as a president who had overcome substantial problems to obtain a position of power.

Both he and his sister frequently heard about their history. Talking about his family's story years later, Winkler said, "I lived with the documentary in my house. My doctor, our cousins, they were all pretty much faux family, because everyone that survived, that met in New York and escaped Hungary or Germany or whatever, became family. So they were all around me." Following the end of the war, the atrocities became much more widely known, and this was another reason that the Jewish community became so much closer in New York, where many of those who fled settled. Their resilience seemed to have had a significant impact on Winkler as well. When talking about the community, he gushed about their fortitude and tenacity because they had, like his parents, started all over again, but with the added disadvantage of not speaking English. He then said, "Maybe I inherited that sense of tenacity." This is possible as life was not easy for Winkler, a son of whom his parents had high expectations. Growing up in a large Jewish community, he was raised with a similar mindset and to honor the traditions, but they were not kosher (they didn't strictly follow Jewish law, so they had a different diet and activities).

His sister was a good student, and he was expected

to excel in his studies as well. Unfortunately for Winkler, he proved to be a very poor student, and it was decades before he learned the reason why. However, he was expected to do much better than he was doing in school. He later said of his childhood in the 1950s and 1960s, "When I was growing up, no one knew what learning challenges were. So, I was called 'stupid,' 'lazy,' and 'not living up to my potential' because he was very verbal, and I guess I had a sense of humor." The fact that he seemed to be able to comprehend and speak made people think that he was intentionally failing at subjects because he simply wasn't taking them seriously. Having no idea that there was anything wrong with his ability to learn, Winkler participated in a wide range of activities where he was able to find success. One of the times when he remembers being successful when he was young, was when he won a dance contest while attending a school for boys. This seemed to have been one of the inspirations for his future career; "That did give me a sense of belonging. But I wanted to be an actor, and I wasn't even able to do some of the school plays because my grades were so low I wasn't allowed to participate in extracurricular activities."

With his parents being somewhat cruel to him at home and his school seeming to shame him during the day, Winkler suffered from extremely low self-esteem. It seemed he really took the criticisms seriously, and he wondered, along with everyone else, why he failed in school. However, he also knew that he was trying. His grades and efforts simply seemed to be inadequate. With so many people putting the blame on him, there was no evidence just how hard he actually was working, leading him to feel like an outsider; "Inside you feel one way, and people are telling you that you are another way, and I couldn't reconcile that."

There were some people who were supportive, seeing his efforts and wanting to foster those efforts as he grew. One teacher in particular, Mr. Rock, knew that Winkler had potential because he was so creative. While so many people were telling him he would not make anything of himself if he didn't work harder, Mr. Rock told Winkler that he could find success. When asked why his music teacher stood out so much, Winkler responded, "He was an adult who was quiet enough to see the actual human being in front of him, and not who he expected the person to be. Children have multiple layers; they are what they show you on the outside, and the depth of their greatness is on the inside."

His strict and demanding parents did a lot of lasting damage to their young son because they did not seem to show him any support. They nicknamed him "Shtum Hund" and "Dumm Hund," which both translate to "dumb dog." One time when his efforts seemed to be particularly egregious, his parents ordered him to his room, then made him remain there for six weeks. They believed that forcing him to stay in his room to study would improve his grades, which was an effort that clearly failed as the problem wasn't that he was unwilling to learn, but he was unable to learn through traditional means. Their cruelty became something that Winkler later actively ensured he did not carry forward to anyone in his life, especially his own children when he had them. Knowing he had a learning disability would likely have changed his parents' approach, but they lived in a time when the way people learned wasn't understood, and learning disabilities were not even a trait people knew to look for in children. It was one of his earliest challenges and one that helped him become one of the most beloved people in Hollywood. Nor did he appear to hold it against his parents because he understood how things had been for them, and it wasn't that they were terrible people, there just wasn't the same understanding about how people learn as there is today.

CHAPTER 3

His early education was fraught with difficulties that continued up to the end of high school. When it came time to graduate from McBurney School (his high school), Winkler couldn't attend the ceremony because he still had to go to summer school to retake geometry. It was his fourth time taking the course, and he finally passed it, and that allowed him to graduate the same year in 1963. His diploma was mailed to him, giving him no ceremony to help celebrate what today would be recognized as a substantial achievement.

Even though his grades had been fairly poor, it was expected that he would attend college because his father wanted him to take over the lumber business that his father had built since arriving in the US. His efforts to get into college began his senior year in high school, and the teenage Winkler sent applications to nearly 30 colleges in an effort to see which colleges would accept him. The answer was two: Park University, located in Missouri, and Emerson College, located in Boston, Massachusetts. It doesn't seem that it was a difficult decision for him, but the problems that had plagued his time in high school continued into college. When talking about the experience, Winkler said, "I packed my bags, came up to Boston, nearly flunked out my first year and got kicked out of my drama major in my second year, but I was able to finally graduate." After successfully passing geometry, he headed to college, but he did not major in anything that would help him as a businessman. Instead, he chose to go into the field that he had wanted to enter for a while - he went into acting, and he did earn his theater degree. It also became clear how much he was influenced by his experiences as a child because he minored in child psychology. This, too, came into play when he was considerably older, as well as when he had children of his own to raise.

Winkler may have had trouble with getting his education, but he was fairly adept at making friends because of how gregarious he has always been. He joined the fraternity Alpha Pi Theta, which really helped the fraternity a decade or so later when he became one of their most recognizable alumni. While he was in college, Winkler really seemed to enjoy being in the fraternity. It is considered a social fraternity, and they have stated that their goals are to encourage brotherhood, love, and trust.

It also appears that college was a much better experience than what he had experienced up to that point. There were some definite troubles with the education portion of his time in college, as he pointed out in a single sentence, but he did find that he was able to make friends and finally feel more accepted than he had before college. This might have helped him to get through college, even if he clearly didn't enjoy a lot of the classes nearly as much as it was a career that highlighted his learning disability – something he still didn't know about at the time.

After graduating from Emerson in 1967, he was accepted into the Yale School of Drama, and he graduated with a Master of Fine Arts in 1970. During many of his interviews, he talks about the many different experiences and teachers. Several of the teachers that he worked with during these times helped to influence his acting during the role that finally won him an Emmy many years later. It's well worth going through some of the interviews because Winkler is an incredibly expressive storyteller, making it easy to see the events through his eyes.

CHAPTER 4

Once he had his college degrees, Winkler worked toward becoming a professional actor. This remains one of the most difficult professions for people to become successful. Well aware that this was the case, and given how difficult things had been in school, he knew that he needed to have another career plan in case the acting dream did not come true. He didn't even seem to consider taking over his father's company. Instead, his backup plan pointed toward a desire to help children like him – he planned to become a child psychologist. This is still fairly obvious today because he continues to love children, giving them attention and focusing on them in a way that he wished he had been noticed when he was a child. It's clear that he enjoys the way children see the world during his interactions, so this appears like it could have been a great thing for the children he could have treated. It's also possible it might have been very difficult for him because he would have seen children having extreme difficulty, which is incredibly hard for therapists to see all of the time.

It never got to the point where he found out if he would be a good therapist. He found minor jobs working in commercials, appearing in 30 or so in the early part of his career. Just four years after graduating from college, he was given a major role in a movie, *The Lords of Flatbush*. He had a few other small parts in other shows and TV, but his next big role came later that year (1973) when he was cast to play a charismatic character on a new show set in the 1950s. This was his huge break because the show was *Happy Days*, and he played a greaser called Arthur Fonzarelli, more commonly called Fonzie on the show. Airing on ABC, the role was initially a small one because the people running the show were afraid that their audience would perceive him as being a little reckless, more of a hoodlum than someone the audience could connect with. Clearly, the executives did not understand their audience because the squeaky-clean family who was supposed to be the main focus, especially their teenage son (played by Ron Howard), was not as popular or well-liked as Fonzie. Winkler's role grew increasingly bigger as people in 1970s were definitely able to relate more to the greaser, who better matched the mindset at the times.

While not as obviously beloved as Fonzie, the primary family was still well-loved, and the show really started to take off. There may have been some sense of nostalgia as it played on the lifestyles of a couple of decades past, but many of the people watching were too young to remember the 1950s. While the parents wanted to watch shows like this with their children, the younger generations were drawn to the character who was more of a rebel. The more popular the show became, the more people wanted to see Fonzie.

There was definitely something incredibly charismatic about the character as well. He appeared to be very laidback and ready to get whatever he wanted, but that was tempered by an apparent understanding of the world. His dark brown hair was large and styled in a way unlike most of the other characters on the show. With his signature leather jacket and signature thumbs up, Fonzie stole nearly every scene he appeared in. He often held up his thumbs and said "Aayyy" in a way that was fun to imitate. The fact that he also rode a motorcycle gave him a certain kind of appeal as people sought more freedom, an independence that is associated with this particular type of vehicle.

What is incredibly ironic about the role is that Fonzie was young and had an effortless confidence that allowed him to snap his fingers and get his way. While this was clearly what the script called for, Winkler's portrayal was what made it seem believable, especially when it came to women. Fonzie could snap his fingers and get women to do what he wanted them to do, something he later laughed about, saying that would have the opposite effect in real life. The character's personality was also completely different from what life had been like for Winkler. He had what he called "high level of low self-esteem," so he couldn't really identify with the character's perspective from his own experiences. It just showed how well he was able to analyze characters so that he was able to act in a way that was very different from his own personality and experiences.

People who met Winkler in real life at this time probably felt he was very much like his character. While many actors who suddenly found themselves in such popular roles became egotistical and unrelatable in real life, Winkler didn't seem to change at all. This partly demonstrates how separate he was from his character because he appreciated his fans. It also showed that he was able to handle stardom without becoming an impossible diva. Perhaps because of his character's popularity and recognition, Winkler also became even more polite – this is very likely a sign of how much he appreciated how people viewed him, as well as a great understanding that it was the fans who really helped him to find astronomical success that few actors ever achieve. He did not take it for granted, and that likely helped to make people love him even from his early days as a successful actor.

As the show continued to change, the focus eventually shifted to Fonzie. When he was made to be so impossibly cool that he could water ski and then jump over a shark, this came to be a sign that the show had outlived its lifespan. Ron Howard had left the show a while before that point, and the people behind the scenes seemed unable to figure out what to do next. Known as "jumping the shark," this strange addition and climax to an episode made it clear that the show was not going to last much longer.

Happy Days was finally cancelled in 1984. Since he had played an iconic character, it probably seemed inevitable that he would become a huge actor, finding roles in whatever he wanted to be in. Unfortunately, that was not the case. Like many people who start their career with a large, popular role, it seemed to define who he was and what he could do. Nearly 40 years old when the show ended, Winkler started to make a shift in his focus. However, by this time he had learned something important about himself, meaning that he was also actively working to find other successes with his recognized learning disability.

CHAPTER 5

In 1978 Winkler married Stacey Weitzman, who already had a son by a previous relationship. It doesn't appear that Winkler had any trouble treating his stepson as his own, taking a lot of interest in the boy's abilities and skills. Given his own history, Winkler was concerned that his stepson, Jed, was incredibly verbal and creative, but was not performing up to his potential with his grades. It seemed incredibly incongruent with how he acted, and Winkler was already aware that grades did not reflect a person's abilities or indicate their level of effort. Despite being clearly adept, Jed wasn't able to express himself in reports, largely because he had so much trouble writing, both in the lettering and getting his ideas down on paper (back then reports were all done with pen and paper). By the late 1970s and early 1980s, medical professionals and educators were starting to realize that there were learning disabilities that made it harder for some children to learn in classes. When Jed was tested to determine if he had one of the recognized issues, they found that he had dyslexia.

Dyslexia is considered a decoding disorder, or a disability that makes it difficult for the person with the disorder from being able to identify sounds and letters written on the page. There are different types and degrees of the problem, with some people seeing letters reflected in a different direction or appearing in a different order. The root cause of the problem is in the brain, where written language is not properly processed. It is not a reflection of intelligence or abilities, as his parents and educators had constantly told him. Anyone with this disorder can be just as successful as other people; they just need tutoring and help to understand how things are meant to be interpreted. Studies have also shown that providing emotional support is incredibly important for people with this disorder because they are often already very frustrated and upset because they cannot see the problem or comprehend why they aren't able to understand. When given emotional support, children and young adults are much more likely to be able to overcome the problem and learn how to learn. This is why early assessment is strongly recommended for children who seem to be having trouble with learning but not in any other areas of their life. When it is determined that they do have dyslexia, children can go through an intervention that will ensure they can reach their full potential without enduring years of fighting through the problem alone. Even if it is determined that an adult has dyslexia, though, it is possible to help them learn how to work through the problem. Even knowing that there is a disorder behind the learning problems can help people feel better. One of the primary symptoms of the disorder is that it is very difficult for a person to read and write. This can lead to mispronunciations and difficulty learning new words since we tend to learn new words through reading when we get older. It is also much more difficult to learn a new language, and it can affect a person's math skills.

Learning that his stepson had dyslexia and that all of his symptoms were so similar to the ones Winkler had experienced as a child, it started to become clear just why learning had always seemed almost impossible. At 31 years old, Winkler finally learned that he was dyslexic, and the reading disorder had caused a lot of his problems, in part because so many people blamed him for his learning difficulties. As he commented during an interview a couple of decades later, "...everything that they said about Jed was true about me. And I realized, oh, I'm not a stupid dog. I actually have something with a name." This is a common reaction with people who have suffered from a disease or disorder, but were blamed for their difficulties.

When asked about how helpful it was to finally have a reason for the issues, Winkler's initial reaction is incredibly understandable, "I got very angry because all of that – all of the arguments in my house with the short Germans who were my parents were for naught. All of the grounding was for naught. Then I .... I am in the bottom 3%, academically, in America. That is calculated. And then I went from all of that anger to. I now understand, possibly, if I didn't fight through my dyslexia, I would not be sitting at this microphone chatting with you."

It shows just how well Winkler is able to process and then realize that what he did was incredibly impressive. Not only did he get a Master's degree, he went into a profession where he was required to read a lot. During the same interview, he talked about how he embarrassed himself at the *Happy Days* table Monday read for about a decade because he had trouble reading the script. Since he was having trouble with nearly every single word, he became increasingly more self-conscious and embarrassed. This would have continued to be a problem if he had gone into public speeches or other activities that required regular reading, but actors are expected to memorize their lines. Once he had completed that part of the process, he didn't have any trouble. Since he had been memorizing for years by this point, Winkler did not have trouble retaining what he memorized, saying, "My brain is then able to suck it up like a vacuum cleaner."

It does not appear to have changed his opinion of his parents, whom he admitted he really didn't like. While he considered them religious, he was much less strict about following Judaism. Part of this may have been because of the way they treated him. He has stated that he thought that the way they treated him and the disappointment in him was much more likely just who they were, and they expected more of him because of who they were, not what they had undergone.

After coming to terms with how dyslexia had affected his life, Winkler was able to use what he had learned to become a proponent for those who have the disorder.

CHAPTER 6

By the time Happy Days ended, Winkler was already aware of his disorder. This should have helped him to find new roles, but he quickly learned that no one wanted to hire someone so attached to a popular character. Just like the people behind the scenes had misidentified how people would feel about Fonzie, these same people thought that he couldn't play any other role because audiences would only see Fonzie. Essentially, people didn't want to hire Fonzie, clearly failing to understand the nature of acting. For nearly a decade, he was unable to get acting work because of this ridiculous bias. While it did upset him that people didn't see him as being capable of being anything else, he never got upset at Happy Days, nor did he think that it ruined his career. To this day, he still remains grateful for his time on the show, and he is close to many of the people he worked with on set. It's even possible that some of the roles that he got later were because of his connections with people like Ron Howard. Howard was one of the producers of Arrested Development, as well as being the narrator on the show. Winkler wound up as one of the least cool characters on the show – Barry, the lawyer, was nothing like Fonzie.

However, the lack of acting roles did have a detrimental effect on Winkler, as acting was what he loved to do. When talking about it decades later, he said, "I was typecast. I had psychic pain that was debilitating because I didn't know what to do. I didn't know where to find it, whatever it was, I didn't know what I was going to do. I had a family. I had a dog. I had a roof." Still, he has said he wouldn't have traded his time on *Happy Days* for anything because he loved working with the people and getting to travel.

It wasn't that he was entirely without offers to try out for other roles. He was initially asked if he wanted to play Danny Zuko, the main male lead in *Grease*, because he was so closely associated with that type of role. Going from Fonzie to Danny would have made a lot of sense, but he turned it down because he didn't want to always play the same roles. Eventually, the role went to John Travolta.

Without any roles that really piqued his interest, Winkler decided to make a move that is incredibly common for people who have managed to make a name for themselves in the industry – he moved behind the scenes. In some ways, it's actually a way to shift the power dynamic because he would now be one of the people who had say over what was going to happen. In 1985, he started a production company, meaning that he was able to control things in a way that he probably wouldn't have been able to without his iconic role. He may have become typecast, but he had gained enough popularity and fame that he was able to do something incredibly difficult. It is also a huge gamble. What is perhaps a bit ironic is that he was very much more attuned to what audiences wanted to see, which became clear with the first show that his company produced, the hit series *MacGyver*. The show was wildly popular in the 1980s and early 1990s as it followed a man who was able to get out of nearly any situation through skill and intelligence. This was often spoofed in other shows, especially *Saturday Night Live*, but that did not detract from how entertaining the show was. There were other shows like *The A Team* and *Magnum PI* that had similar concepts, but a very different execution of the concept. *MacGyver* went on to win five Emmys during its seven-year run. This could very likely have been why Winkler's memories of his first show weren't tainted by being typecast – he was able to learn from the mistakes and misconceptions of producers to be highly successful in Hollywood.

CHAPTER 7

I t took nearly a decade after the show ended, but people finally started hiring "The Fonz" because there were new people in power. Perhaps one of the most recognizable and notable of those who wanted to have Winkler in their work was Wes Craven. His name and rise in popularity had been fairly quick as the man behind A Nightmare on Elm Street, and he had become synonymous with the horror genre. However, his influence had also waned since the release of the first Nightmare movie in 1984, the same year that Happy Days was canceled. It seems that Craven knew he wanted Winkler in the role, so he approached the man who hadn't had many acting roles over the last decade and requested he take a role in a horror movie that was in the works. It would be an uncredited role that wasn't meant to take up much time as it was a relatively small part. Essentially, Winkler's character, Principal Himbry, was there to pad the body count, but true to the nature of the slasher movie, there was a lot of meta moments in the movie. By getting "The Fonz" to play a completely different type of role, Craven was getting yet another reference he could add to a movie chock-full of callbacks and references.

Winkler didn't seem to have a problem being uncredited, so he accepted a role that was well outside of his usual experience. One of the reasons given for not adding his name was that though more than a decade had passed since he had played Fonzie, Winkler was still a household name. By not putting his name on the screen, Craven thought that the younger actors would get more attention. Craven was not a man for doing things by the book, and in that same movie, he killed off the person who was arguably the most notable name in the film, Drew Barrymore, within the first scene of the movie. This highlighted the way he was bringing new blood to the forefront – which he had done with *Nightmare*, the first major role of Johnny Depp. This suited Winkler, probably because he was just happy to get back in front of the camera, even if it was for a role that was entirely unlike anything he had previously done.

His character spends most of his time in the principal's office reprimanding students and dealing with the fear students felt after the murder of two of their own. At one point, he hears something and sticks his head out of the door. He says something, causing a janitor mopping the floor to look up.

Anyone who knows anything about Craven's work automatically recognized the janitor, wearing a red striped sweater and a fedora, which was a reference to Freddy Kreuger, the killer from the *Nightmare* movies. Craven himself played the character, making it stand out that much more. And if there was any question about the nod to Craven's earlier work, Himbry says, "Not you, Fred," which makes it clear that this was one of the many Easter eggs in the movie. Himbry continued to walk around his office, yanking open the door to his closet, and for a moment, eagle-eyed viewers will see a leather jacket hanging up just in sight of the camera. Within a short span of time, Craven had added two things that people could easily associate with both his history in the industry and Winkler's history. It was a really nice touch that made the already fantastic movie that much more enjoyable.

Although it was short, Winkler commented that one part of the scene took an incredibly long time to film. "This one shot, with the bad guy with the mask coming into my eyeball, it took two hours to shoot. As he was stabbing me, Wes, in his professional way, came up and he said, 'Do you think it might be more excruciating? Do you think being stabbed you would scream a little louder?' I said I could do that." It's entertaining to consider what it would have been like for Winkler because something that seems obvious is actually much harder to imagine doing in a movie since it's clearly not real. Also, there's a fear of being too loud and hurting the ears of people around you.

From there, he started to appear in a much wider array of work, including the comedy *The Waterboy* in 1998 and the TV show *Arrested Development* as an inept lawyer. This found him a whole new fanbase in younger generations who were less familiar with his work as Fonzie, while showing others that he was able to take on roles that were very different from his iconic role. His turn on *Arrested Development* had him referencing the Fonz at one point when he held a comb and lifted his hands up while looking in a mirror, a move that was one of Fonzie's signature moves. As he started to get a lot more work back in front of the screen, Winkler found himself getting the kind of attention that is rare for older actors. He had a new fanbase, which also helped to bring *Happy Days* back into the social consciousness too. People who saw him in the newer roles were interested in seeing the role that helped launch his career. That meant that it was that much easier to have the little Easter Eggs calling back to it as time went by because more and more people were able to understand the reference.

CHAPTER 8

As he became a more regular TV figure, Winkler finally started to get offers for more roles. He appeared in many TV and films as minor characters and recurring characters. He also ended up getting cast on a wide range of popular shows, such as Parks and Recreation and BoJack Horseman. Looking at the last 20 years of his career, it is far more varied and full of credits than any other period of his career. It was like seeing him doing something beyond playing a greaser made people realize he was an actor, which meant he was able to occupy many different characters with great results. Between the beginning of 2021 and the middle of 2023, he had roughly two dozen credits to his name – and that was credits, not his uncredited roles.

It was when another actor started taking a similar trajectory – he wanted to break out of his comedy roles and move into more work behind the scenes at the same time – that Winkler was given his next major role that made use of his talents.

Winkler said that he was driving somewhere when he got a call about a new upcoming role. His agent told him that he was wanted to audition for a role with Bill Hader, and she told him that he was on the shortlist. He has said that he immediately responded "yes," but he also said during his NPR interview that his reaction was "Bill Hader, *Saturday Night Live.* And it's HBO. HBO?" When she let him know that he had it right, he asked her a more pressing question, "And then I said, OK. I'm on a shortlist. Is Dustin Hoffman on that list? Because if he is, I'm not going in because he's getting it." It was only when he was assured that the Oscar winner wasn't one of the people on the list, he wanted to review the script and go to the audition. When it came time for him to audition, it was his youngest son, who had become a director, who helped him to get through the scenes for the audition. The extra work paid off because he said that he managed to make Hader laugh during that first audition. The wait for a callback was painful as Winkler was excited about the possible role. Since Hader was working on doing more than just comedy, he was doing a lot of the work, including a good bit of the writing. When he finished writing two more scenes, he again called Winkler and asked if he wanted to come in to try them. Winkler's gut reaction was kept in his head because he did *not* want to go in and do another round. He had successfully made someone who had been instrumental during a successful age of *Saturday Night Live* laugh on his first try. He was afraid that he wouldn't be able to accomplish the same effect, meaning he might not get chosen for the role. However, his verbal response was to say, "Of course I want to come in. Just send me the script."

That was the start of a resurgence as he took on a regular supporting role that helped him become more than a charismatic character who could do no wrong. The show *Barry* is considered a dark comedy (airing a year before Hader was cast in the horror movie *It Chapter Two*) that stretched both Hader and Winkler's skills because it was a very different version of what they had played in previous roles. The show is about a marine named Barry Berkman who becomes a hitman. When he travels to kill one of his targets in LA, he joins an acting class taught by Gene Cousineau. Winkler plays the acting teacher, and he has been incredibly important in the show, providing a supporting actor role that won him an Emmy. The show was very well-received and won numerous awards over its four seasons. Winkler's character seems to become more of a father figure to Barry, who spends a lot of time dealing with underworld characters over the course of the show. It's a strange dynamic, especially as Cousineau really doesn't care about his students. As a narcissistic, eccentric actor, he has managed to alienate himself from many of the people within the industry. Their relationship does not continue on good terms when Barry kills someone close to Cousineau. While it takes on some serious topics, the show still has a lot of comedic elements that keep the tone from getting too dark.

Winkler has gushed about his time on the show, expressing how much he loves the writers and other people behind the scenes. As one of the writers, actors, producers, and sometimes director, Hader had a lot of control over production, and he had a "No A-holes on set" policy that included the actors. Winkler has even said that the show made him a better actor because it made him do new things. When the show ended, it was emotional for him because he knew it had to end, but he was sad that he had to say goodbye to everyone. He has been just as effusive about how wonderful the crew was as he was about the other actors. This is the reputation he has had in the industry pretty much since the 1970s when he first rose to fame.

CHAPTER 9

While the beginning of his life was very difficult and he didn't feel supported, once he was on his own and establishing his career, Winkler seems to have established the kind of family that he wished he had experienced while he was growing up. Having never felt like he was a proper member of the family, or at least feeling like he could never be the son his parents wanted, Winkler once recalled, "As a child, before I went to bed, I thought every night that I would be a different parent from my parents." He goes on to recount how he couldn't understand his fellow students when they talked about going places with their families or having a great time with their parents. He had spent so much time being punished for not living up to their expectations that he could not see them in this kind of light. What his treatment seems to have done was to teach him that there was another way for parents and children to interact, and that was the way he wanted to interact with his children. He couldn't have learned this from his grandparents because he never knew them, as they died in concentration camps before he was born.

For him, a new opportunity at family life came along in 1976. Stacey Weitzman attended the University of Southern California and later started a public relationship firm. When Winkler entered, she was at one of her clients' places of business, Jerry Magnin's clothing store. By this time, he had been on *Happy Days* and was easily recognizable. Not long after entering the shop, someone called out, "Hey, there's Fonzie," drawing the attention of everyone in the place to the actor. He returned a week later and found that she was also there. Soon they went out for ginger ales, and that led to them really getting along well. Two years later, they married. They held their ceremony at a synagogue in Winkler's hometown, New York City. She later admitted that having such a famous husband was difficult; "People would rush up to Henry and literally walk over my feet. One time I said, 'You've just completely ruined my stockings.' And this woman said, 'But I love Fonzie!'" Despite the trials of the early days, the two settled into a much more comfortable norm. This included her son Jed, who was four years old when the couple first met.

Two years after they married, they had their first child together, whom they named Zoe. Three years later, they had their second child, whom they named Max. Winkler always talks about his three children, demonstrating that he understands that family doesn't have to be blood-related to be family. Their willingness to help was demonstrated when they met Marlee Matlin when she was just 12 years old. She is a gifted actress who is also deaf. When she was 20 years old, she asked the Winklers if she could stay with them for a few days because she was having some trouble. Those few days ended up stretching into nearly three years. Winkler has reportedly said that he thinks of her as his second daughter, having helped her through a difficult time when she had to deal with many different issues, including alcoholism. During this time, she also met the man who later became her husband, expanding the family further.

Winkler and his wife are among the longest-established couples in Hollywood, which she has attributed to growing together instead of allowing themselves to drift apart. People do not stay the same as they age, and that is definitely true after marrying. The couple did not allow their marriage to be compromised as they changed over the years. By working to keep their relationship intact, they were able to have a healthy, happy relationship for decades. She recognizes that it isn't always easy, but as long as you focus on what's important and remember what you love about your partner, the friendship that is developed can help keep focus on what matters.

Winkler has spoken at length about how he wanted to have the kind of father he wanted to be, using his parents as a template of how not to parent a child. He wanted to make sure his children always felt seen and heard, as well as having good memories of their parents.

Since he did go into acting, Winkler ended up taking up his other interest in children in a more philanthropic way. Working with his wife, they established the Children's Action Network. This has been one of the big parts of their lives, giving them a common goal as well. The couple worked with six other couples to found the organization (including Steven Spielberg), making the organization a much more notable endeavor. The focus of the organization is to ensure that children everywhere have access to vaccines, ensuring that children can get them for free, regardless of their situation. Given that he was named after Roosevelt, it could be that he had some sway over his desire to focus on vaccinations. Roosevelt had been a great athlete when he was young, but when he contracted Polio as an adult, the future president never fully recovered, despite the fact that his family was wealthy and could afford the best medication and treatment. The problem was that Polio was a disease that left many children dead and many more disabled. Had vaccinations been available, Roosevelt could have remained healthy.

By the 2020s, the couple had become grandparents to numerous grandbabies. Both of them tend to gush about how much they love spending time with the next generation. They have also been rather comical when talking about how the dynamic is much different because grandparents don't have to be the bad guys – all they have to do is call the parents, and it's the parents who are at fault for the children not being able to do something they want to do.

CHAPTER 10

A s if becoming an actor wasn't already hard enough for someone with dyslexia, Winkler has also become a coauthor (working with Lin Oliver), with many of his books being written for kids. It goes to show that he very much did have the tenacity and willpower to make the best out of a difficult situation. He has also used his writing to help children since many of his books are for kids.

His first book was published not long after becoming a household name. By 1976, he had already lived long enough to be able to write a book of memoirs, which he titled *The Other Side of Henry Winkler*. In 2003, he published his first children's book, and he has become a prolific children's author since then, completing several dozen books over the years. He has written two more books that are autobiographical (*I've Never Met an Idiot on the River* and *Being Henry: The Fonz ... and Beyond*), but the vast majority of his stories are made specifically for kids.

When he started writing children's books, he created a character named Hank Zipzer, and he has turned this into a series. The child is like Winkler in that he has dyslexia. This introduces kids to the idea that reading is for everyone, even those who have learning disabilities. He writes the books with Lin Oliver, and they both want to spread the idea of how enjoyable reading is.

Winkler goes on tours to promote his books regularly, reading in front of children. His charisma and personality are perfect for these high-energy engagements because he is able to connect with children in a way that shows how much of a natural parental figure he is. It also shows just how well he was able to learn how to treat children in the way he wished he had been treated. He's an amazing example of how someone who endured abuse as a child (in this case, the way his parents treated him would be considered emotional abuse) goes on to become empathetic and caring.

Even though his parents did not treat him well as a child, he showed care and compassion to his mother after he had found success in acting. In 1989, she suffered a stroke, which affected the use of her arms and caused her pain. At the time, he was working in California, but she was still living in New York. Instead of moving her, he split his time, traveling to his hometown to help take care of her. He has even admitted that he felt guilty that he wasn't there to take care of her all of the time, leaving her to be taken care of by others when he was working. Both he and his sister worked to help their mother, but she had apparently given up on herself. He later commented that it was like watching the life slowly ebb from her, with no one having the ability to stop it. She was no longer the person she had once been, and every day was painful. Since she required regular use of a wheelchair, she stopped leaving her house because she was embarrassed that she couldn't walk normally. It was a slow death as she stopped doing so many things. She finally died in 1998. Having spent so much time taking care of her, Winkler said that he found a new respect for caregivers because he learned first-hand just how hard it is to do it that every day. He also has become an advocate for stroke awareness, particularly for those who suffered from upper limb spasticity, which is what made it difficult for his mother to use her arms.

Over the course of his career, Winkler has participated in numerous Public Service Announcements, better known as PSAs. Since he played a cool yet wise person on *Happy Days*, people were very likely to listen to him in the early days of his career. In 1984, he participated in a PSA called Strong Kids, Safe Kids. During the roughly 40-minute show, he appeared as both The Fonz and as Henry Winkler, one looking cool as he cleaned his motorcycle, and the other a very dad-like figure in his bulky sweater hanging out by a picket fence in front of his house. He was asked to help raise awareness about eye disease as one company started to ramp up the use of a drug that could help. Winkler agreed, largely because his father-in-law had to retire from being a dentist because of his failing eyesight. During the COVID-19 pandemic, he talked with a member of CBS News about social distancing and the rapid shift in life. Initially, he stood at his full glass door, looking out at the world, something that most people could identify with at the time. The correspondent talking to him, Tracy Smith, even said at the beginning of the interview, "I feel like I'm admiring you through a shop window?" His reaction was to hold up his hands to his bright yellow sweater and say, "My sweater?" This got both of them giggling. After taking a few steps back so that there was at least 6 feet between her and Winkler, he opened the door and they chatted about how things had changed, including a disruption to the filming of *Barry*. They quickly moved on to talking about the way he spent time with his grandkids during that troubling time, with him standing at the door and them hanging back on the driveway to see him. They continued speaking on the topic, with Winkler even pulling out his phone to hold it up for the camera to see one of his grandkids dressed up for Halloween. Though the face was blurred out, it was clear that his grandkid

was wearing Winkler's iconic outfit for the holiday –
his grandchild was dressed as Fonzie. Winkler said,
"I didn't know he was going to do this. My heart flew
out of my body when I walked in the house. If my
heart could leave my body and just soar, it would've."
Those kinds of touching moments were disrupted
because of COVID, but he was able to keep his sense
of humor and make Smith laugh as they chatted. It
was a rare scene of normalcy with some odd twists,
demonstrating the importance of being careful, but
also showing that things could still be fun.

CONCLUSION

A handful of actors in Hollywood are known as nice guys, the kind of people who are incredibly approachable and lovable, not taking their stardom for granted. Henry Winkler is one of the few who has proven that the decades of success and stardom did nothing to change who he is or the way he interacts with his fans. His parents were fortunate enough to escape the Holocaust, but they did not foster the kind of support for their child that one might expect from someone who narrowly escaped death. They were cruel to him, in large part because there was no awareness of learning disorders during the majority of the 20th century. Winkler decided to take a different path than his parents had expected of him, and he found success incredibly early, ending up as one of the most recognizable TV characters of all time. Instead of letting that go to his head, Winkler used the platform to be a genuinely nice guy who started helping others. This is something that he continues to do to this day. If there is a cause that he connects with, Winkler seems to be eager to help. However, children's health and wellness seem to be the causes closest to his heart, whether they are his children, the children of friends, or unknown children who need help. He is one of those few inspirational figures who always seems to have an easy smile and kind words. And he always seems happy to give people who recognize him two thumbs up and an "Aayyy" if it will make them smile.

Made in United States
Orlando, FL
01 November 2023

38489757R00033